Sharks!

Anne Schreiber

NATIONAL GEOGRAPHIC
Washington, D.C.

To Ben, who taught me to love unlovable animals.
—A.S.

Published by the National Geographic Society, Washington, D.C. 20036. All rights reserved.
Reproduction in whole or in part without written permission of the publisher is strictly prohibited.

Schreiber, Anne.
Sharks! / by Anne Schreiber.
p. cm. — (National Geographic readers)
ISBN 978-1-4263-0286-2 (paperback) — ISBN 978-1-4263-0288-6 (library binding)
1. Sharks--Juvenile literature. I. Title.
QL638.9.S292 2008
597.3—dc22
2007044161

Printed in the United States of America

Table of Contents

CHOMP!

What is quick?
What is quiet?
What has five rows of teeth?
What glides through the water?
CHOMP!
It's a shark!

Sharks live in all of Earth's oceans.
They have been here for a long time.
Sharks were here before dinosaurs.

OCEANIC WHITETIP SHARK

CARTILAGE: Cartilage is light, strong, and rubbery. The tip of your nose is cartilage. Can you feel how soft it is?

Shark tail fins are larger on top. This helps them move through the water better.

HAMMERHEAD SHARK

A shark is a fish. But a shark is not like other fish. Sharks do not have bones. They have soft cartilage instead. Cartilage helps sharks twist and turn. Cartilage helps sharks move and bend.

If a shark loses a tooth, a new one moves forward to take its place.

Shark skin feels bumpy and rough. It's hard like sandpaper. It protects sharks and helps them swim faster.

Shark Pups

Shark babies are called pups. Some pups grow inside their mothers. Other pups hatch from eggs.

LEMON SHARK

Lemon shark pups grow inside their mothers. The lemon shark mother goes to shallow water to give birth. The pups stay near the shallow water until they are grown.

These fish are called remoras. They hang around sharks and eat their leftovers.

LEMON SHARK PUP

MERMAID'S PURSE

Swell shark pups hatch from eggs. The mother sharks lay the eggs in hard cases. People call the case a mermaid's purse.

A pup coming out of its egg case.

SWELL SHARK PUP

Swell shark mothers lay up to five egg cases at a time. In nine months, the swell shark pups are born.

Pups Grow Up

NURSE SHARK

WORD BITES

PREDATORS: Animals that eat other animals.
PREY: Animals that are eaten by other animals.

When shark pups grow up, they are awesome predators. They have many ways to sense their prey. Did you know a shark can smell blood from miles away? It can smell one drop of blood in 25 million drops of ocean.

Sharks can see better than humans can. Even in deep, dark water, a shark can see its prey.

Sharks take a test bite of prey before eating. Their taste buds tell them if the prey is fat enough to eat.

GREAT WHITE SHARK

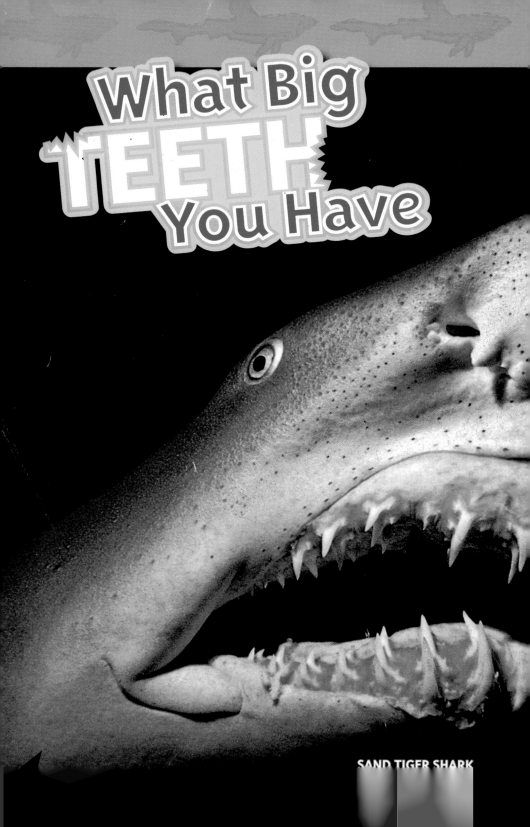

What Big TEETH You Have

SAND TIGER SHARK

Sharks have many rows of teeth.
They are always losing some teeth.
They are always growing new teeth.
A shark uses up more than 10,000
teeth in its life.

Different sharks have different teeth.
Their teeth are perfect for what they eat.

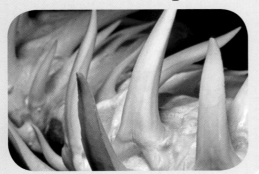

Long, spiky teeth are
for catching.

Flat teeth are for
grinding.

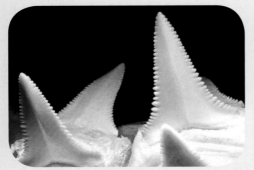

Serrated teeth are
for ripping.

WORD BITES

SERRATED: When something is serrated,
it has a jagged edge, like a saw blade.

WORD BITES

PREHISTORIC: Prehistoric is a time before people wrote things down.
EXTINCT: Extinct plants and animals are no longer alive on Earth.

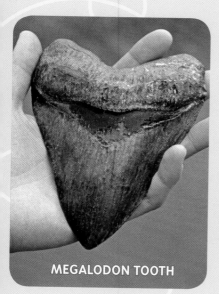

MEGALODON TOOTH

Wow! Prehistoric sharks had really big teeth—up to six inches! Good thing these guys are extinct.

The megalodon is a prehistoric shark. Scientists made a life-sized model of the megalodon's jaw and put in the teeth they have found. You can imagine how big the shark must have been.

Imagine This!

A giant shark is gliding through
the water.
A swimmer is nearby.
The shark gets closer.
It is huge.
It opens its giant mouth and…

WHALE SHARK

…sucks in a big mouthful of water.
The swimmer is fine.
The shark is a whale shark.
Whale sharks are the biggest sharks.
But they have tiny teeth.
They eat tiny animals called plankton.

Blue-Ribbon Sharks

There are about 375 different types of sharks.

1ST PLACE

A hammerhead shark has a head shaped like a giant hammer. Its wide head is great for hunting.

WEIRDEST
The Hammerhead Shark

The spined pygmy shark is about eight inches long. It has a glow-in-the-dark belly.

1ST PLACE

SMALLEST
The Spined Pygmy Shark

When a great white bites its prey, its eyes roll back into its head. This protects its eyes.

CREEPIEST
The Great White Shark

The mako is the fastest shark. It can swim up to 20 miles per hour. Makos leap clear out of the water to catch prey.

FASTEST
The Mako Shark

23

Now You See Them...

LANTERN SHARK

Some sharks glow in the dark! Do you see something shiny in the water? Watch out! The tiny lantern shark is covered with a glow-in-the-dark slime.

The lantern shark is a deep-sea shark. Many deep-sea animals glow. Scientists think glowing might help predators attract prey.

Most sharks are hard to see. They have a dark back. From above, they blend in with the water. They have a white belly. From below, they blend in with the sky.

WOBBEGONG SHARK

Some sharks have special ways to hide.
Wobbegongs have colors like the seafloor.
Their mouths have parts that look
like seaweed. Fish swim in but they can't
get out!

Shark Attack!

One day Bethany Hamilton went surfing. Suddenly, a tiger shark attacked. It tugged her as she held onto her surfboard. It took a big bite out of her surfboard. It also took Bethany's left arm.

After the attack, Bethany wanted to keep surfing. She is not afraid to go in the water. She knows that shark attacks are rare.

Bethany says, "One thing hasn't changed — and that's how I feel when I'm riding a wave."

People Attack?

Shark attacks are scary, and terrible. Sharks can be a danger to people. But people are a bigger danger to sharks. Millions of sharks die in nets set to catch other fish. Others are killed on purpose.

Many types of sharks may become extinct. Sharks have been on Earth for millions of years. Sharks and people need to learn to share the sea.

GRAY REEF SHARK

CARTILAGE
Cartilage is light, strong and rubbery. Shark skeletons are made of cartilage.

EXTINCT
Extinct plants and animals are no longer alive on Earth.

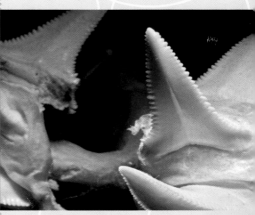

PREDATOR
A predator is an animal that eats other animals.

PREY
Prey are animals that are eaten by other animals.

PREHISTORIC
Prehistoric is a time before people wrote things down.

SERRATED
When something is serrated, it has a jagged edge.